Libido Boost

GABRIEL TOP

Contents

Contents 3
Introduction 5
Birth Control and Your Libido 8
So How can you Increase Your Libido? 12
Libido When You are A couple 15
Being Thrown into Menopause with Surgery 19
Contents 25
Introduction 1
Birth Control and Your Libido 4
So How can you Increase Your Libido? 8
Libido When You are A couple 11
Being Thrown into Menopause with Surgery 15

Introduction

This is one of the issues that are not often discussed in the media: lower sex drive, particularly for women, has been and remains a mystery. And yet, it affects many people. Part of the problem is that women's sexuality is a bit more complicated and complex than men's. An author on WebMD writes, *"Unlike men's main sexual complaint, erectile dysfunction, women's biggest sexual problem is caused by a combination of both mental and physical factors, which aren't likely to be cured by merely popping a pill."*

Women between the age 18 and 59, from reaching puberty to menopause, can start experiencing low sex drive. WebMD's article on the matter includes this really neat quote, "One of first things I do in speaking to women who come in with sexual concerns is let them know that there is no normal frequency or set of behaviors and things change with time," says Jan Shifren, MD, an assistant professor at Harvard Medical School. "If it's working for them and/or their partner, there is no problem."

See, this is part of the problem. We do not know how to quantify "high" and "low" sex drives. Every person has their own "norms" and "standards." Every couple will have their own system, their own norm. "But when a woman experiences a significant decrease in interest in sex that is having an effect on her life and is causing distress, then it's considered a problem of low sexual desire or HSDD."

Right? When it becomes problematic and starts causing you issues in the relationship, then it is time to start considering it a problem. "Kingsberg says that sexual desire is more than just an issue of low libido or sex drive. She says sexual drive is the biological component of desire, which is reflected as spontaneous sexual interest including sexual thoughts, erotic fantasies, and daydreams."

Kingsberg also raises an important point: sex drive decreases by age for a lot of people. "That sexual drive declines naturally with age based on physiological factors. But sexual desire also encompasses interpersonal and psychological factors that create a willingness to be sexual."

Then the article includes several reasons that women start to have low sex drive, "Interpersonal relationship issues. Partner performance problems, lack of emotional satisfaction with the relationship, the birth of a child, and becoming a caregiver for a loved one can decrease sexual desire. Sociocultural influences. Job stress, peer pressure, and media images of sexuality can negatively influence sexual desire.

Low testosterone: Testosterone affects sexual drive in both men and women. Testosterone levels peak in women's mid-20s and then steadily decline until menopause, when they drop dramatically.

Medical problems: Mental illnesses such as depression, or medical conditions, such as endometriosis, fibroids, and thyroid disorders, impact a woman's sexual drive both mentally and physically.

Medications: Certain antidepressants (including the new generation of SSRIs), blood pressure lowering drugs, and oral contraceptives can lower sexual drive in many ways, such as decreasing available testosterone levels or affecting blood flow.

Age: Blood levels of androgens fall continuously in women as they age."

Birth Control and Your Libido

It really depends on the medication you take. Some birth control pills lower sex drive, and others do not. It is all about side effects and individual bodies. Your body reacts to different chemicals in unique ways.

But, it seems like it is more likely that the birth control pill can cause lowering of your sex drive.

Lisa*, a 33-year-old Web designer from New York City, blamcs oral contraccptivcs for a ycar-long libido malfunction she experienced after moving in with her now-husband. "When I realized I had no drive at all, I talked to my doctor, who said it was possible that it was the pill" causing the problem. "So I stopped taking it and used a barrier method, and things got really good again."'

Rodewald does not focus on Lisa alone, she writes about this issue being a common one, "Thirty percent of American women suffer from a diminished sex drive, and some experts (as well as non-experts) will tell you that the pill is often to blame. Studies have linked oral contraceptive use to decreased levels of androgens -- the class of hormones, including testosterone, thought to drive both male and female sexuality. Birth control pills also alter a woman's natural estradiol fluctuations (the group of hormones that includes estrogen), which many ob-gyns consider the main source of female libido. When you're on the pill, your hormonal balance changes -- and consequently, your desire for sex might change, too."

But, hang on, remember that every person is different and so it is natural that studies are not agreeing 100% on this issue. Rodewald reflects, "But don't throw out your pills just yet. Many studies have examined the effect of hormonal birth control on sex drive, but few have been conclusive, says Anne R. Davis, MD, MPH, assistant clinical professor of obstetrics and gynecology at Columbia University Medical Center in New York, who published a review of 40 years' worth of literature on contraceptive-libido studies. "

At epigee.org, there is a guide for the birth control pill and its effects on sex drives. The author explains, "It appears that the birth control pill affects sex drive because it acts directly on a woman's sexual hormones. In particular, the birth control pill inhibits the production of androgens, including testosterone, in a woman's ovaries. Androgens have a direct effect on the pleasure that you experience during sexual intercourse.

Additionally, the birth control pill also appears to increase the amount of sex-hormone binding globulin (SHBG) in the body. SHBG is a protein that binds to testosterone, preventing a woman's body from using it effectively. High levels of SHBG have been directly linked to decreased libido and sexual desire."
Just because it affects the sexual hormones does not mean that there is a decrease in it. It just means that it could be increased, decreased, or stay the same.

So How can you Increase Your Libido?

According to an article in Huffingtonpost.com, Shelley Emling writes, "In general, some 43 percent of women and 31 percent of men in the United States report sexual dysfunction. The numbers are even higher for those over 50. Indeed one study of menopausal women found that nearly half reported a decrease in sexual desire after menopause. Lots of issues contribute to the problem, including stress, smoking and hormonal imbalance." There are some ways you can increase your sex drive, though.

Aside from relaxing, changing medication, there are more solid ways to increase your sex drive naturally. "A study by Helen Fisher, an anthropologist at Rutgers University, found that when people look at a photo of their loved one for 30 seconds or longer, their brain begins producing dopamine, a libido booster. Of course, I know a lot of women who'd say that gazing at a photo of Ryan Gosling might be helpful as well."

Not only do you want to look your best, then, but you also need to stay fit for your sex drive naturally. "This one's mostly for men: Not only will you simply feel better about yourself, but body fat also inhibits testosterone production. And, apparently, it's really important for men to watch their waist size as belly fat absorbs testosterone more efficiently than fat cells elsewhere in the body. Both men and women will benefit from exercise, though, as aerobic workouts increase blood flow to sex organs"

Let us go back to relaxing, though, because it is really important to unwind: "No, you shouldn't drink to excess. And don't give up champagne completely. But studies show that moderate drinkers of red wine actually have a greater sex drive than those who don't imbibe, or who drink white wine. Researchers attribute this to red wine's ability to increase blood flow as well as its color. Women apparently find men a whole lot sexier when they are wearing red. And -- no surprise here -- men also are attracted to ladies in red."

Speaking of relaxing, "Certain scents are known to put people in the mood immediately (stock up on cinnamon, vanilla and musk in particular). An interesting side note: A woman's sense of smell is actually stronger than a man's, especially when she's ovulating. When it comes to men, apparently they get turned on by the scent of pumpkin pie combined with lavender. Who knew?"

Of course, I am going to be boring and say that communicating is also a natural way of increasing sex drives naturally. The more you share with your significant other, the better your sex life will be. And have fun: "Recent research shows that partaking in new and challenging experiences with your partner can boost the brain chemical dopamine, which helps fuel sex drive. These don't even need to be in the bedroom. Enter a race together, on a tandem bike. Get a little lost on a wilderness hike—without a map. Host a game night with friends where each couple kicks in $30 and the winning pair takes all," Deborah Kotz writes.

Libido When You are A couple

Sex ties and binds a couple together. It keeps them close. Michele Weiner-Davis writes, "You have to stop thinking you can have a great relationship without satisfying sex unless your partner wholeheartedly agrees. Don't resign yourself to passionless lovemaking or a relationship void of true intimacy. Even elderly and chronically ill people can enjoy a robust sex life."

So, how do you deal with someone who has a lower sex drive? Well, first, rule out any medical issues. Weiner-Davis explains, "To eliminate physiological causes for your lack of desire, a trip to your family physician or gynecologist may be in order. Ask if hormone replacement therapy such as testosterone would be appropriate. Evaluate whether side effects from medications or medical conditions are a factor in your situation. Discuss whether herbal remedies or dietary changes may be helpful."

Next, you may want to talk to a therapist to help you figure out if there is emotionally going on. Weiner-Dennis writes, "If you are a man whose sexual desire has plummeted due to your having sexual problems such as impotence or performance anxiety, a certified sex therapist can teach you many different techniques to overcome these difficulties.
It has been proven that regular and good exercise can among other benefits increase bloodflow to the

penis tissues for men thereby leading to improved sexual performance

Another natural way to increase libido is to get more used to eating Bananas, plantains and the NUTs such as Dates, coconuts, peanuts, tiger nuts and also yogurts. All of these food mentioned food items has over the years been proven helpful in increasing Libido level in both Men and Women.

You might also consider taking a drug such as Viagra, which will help you have and maintain an erection. I know it is really difficult for a man to admit he is worried about low sexual desire and even more difficult to ask for help in this area. But I urge you to do precisely that. You need to put your pride aside and get your sex life/marriage back on track. Your wife may understand at the moment, but if you put things off much longer, she might not be around."

Weiner-Dennis advises you to flirt, "If you think back to earlier times in your relationship, I bet the two of you were more flirtatious. I bet there were pats on the butt, a wink of your eye, a kiss blown across a crowded room, lightly touching each other in passing, a suggestive smile, a well-timed compliment about your spouse's appearance, and so on.

Either of you can initiate a conversation and talk about how romantically hot your first seven sexual intercourse you had together, in bet it was hot, mind-blowing, adventurous pleasurable as my own experience still linger in my head even as I write this book. This kind of playfulness is an important part of keeping passion alive. Put more energy into letting your spouse know that s/he is attractive by flirting."

Okay, so we got flirting, seeking medical and professional help. What else can you do to increase your sex drive? Weiner-Dennis explains, "Dr. Pat Love, coauthor of Hot Monogamy, suggests that it is frequently the case that people with low sexual desire never experience earth-shattering sexual urges as do their more sexually-oriented partners. For them, it's more like barely noticeable, mild tremors. Rather than assume that the Tidal Wave will be the cue that it's "sex time," look for more subtle signs"

And finally, you have to move, run: "Joggers always say that the hardest part about running is putting on your running shoes; so too with sex. I wish I had a dollar for every time I've heard a person say, "I really wasn't in the mood at all at first, but once we got into it, I enjoyed myself." My wife can testify to this. When people nudge themselves, even halfheartedly, to "get their feet moving," their pleasurable physical sensations often override any reason to resist."

Being Thrown into Menopause with Surgery

If you have to have a hysterectomy due to female issues this can really throw your body for a loop, especially if it is a total hysterectomy where they take out both of your ovaries.

Now your body is fighting you for the hormones it has been use to all these years that have been stripped away leaving you with nothing and this entire nothing? That leads to a low or nonexistent libido which of course is going to play havoc in your relationship.

Your partner won't understand why a surgery has taken your from yahoo to ya what in 2.5 seconds. They won't understand why you are tired all the time, why you can't even think about sex; when there isn't that "urge" there you just don't even care.

Know that you are not alone! Millions of women walk into their doctors office every year with a variety of complaints from aches and pains to lack of a sex drive or fatigue and most doctors don't even think about hormones they go right to their typical standbys, anti-anxiety meds, anti-depressants or a variety of medications to treat the symptoms.

If you have had a hysterectomy, are in menopause even if it has been years tell your Dr. you want your hormone levels checked!! I know of a woman who was one of these women who were given anti-anxiety meds and was on them for about 4 years before she read up about hormone replacement and all of the things in your body that are affected by your hormones!

She was 34 when she had a total hysterectomy, threw her into menopause immediately, was on a hormone patch for a couple years but it didn't really work too well. Hormones for women are a mix of Testosterone, Estrogen and Progesterone and all of these need to be at the right levels in order for you to feel your best!

Most Doctors don't have the perfect combination to give you and it's trial and error but there are those out there that will get your current levels and give you what you need to get to where you need to be and it is something that is inserted so you are never without! Once they know what you need and how often that is how often you will go in and get the pellets inserted.

She was going every 8 weeks, but everyone is different, some can go for months! Do yourself and your partner a favor and if you don't have a partner do it for you!! she did! she has been married for over 25 years and the difference between having the hormone replacement and not having it is like night and day!

Sex is sweet and it plays a vital role in every marriage, you do not have to starve your partner of sex, keep your home stay sexy.

Peace peace peace

Libido Boost

Whether you are a man or a woman having a low libido isn't any fun for anyone but how do

LIBIDO
BOOST
INCREASE YOUR
SEX DRIVE
TODAY!

you boost it? Here are some tips and ideas for getting your libido back!

GABRIEL TOP

Contents

Contents 3
Introduction 5
Birth Control and Your Libido 8
So How can you Increase Your Libido? 12
Libido When You are A couple 15
Being Thrown into Menopause with Surgery 19
Contents 25
Introduction 1
Birth Control and Your Libido 4
So How can you Increase Your Libido? 8
Libido When You are A couple 11
Being Thrown into Menopause with Surgery 15

Introduction

This is one of the issues that are not often discussed in the media: lower sex drive, particularly for women, has been and remains a mystery. And yet, it affects many people. Part of the problem is that women's sexuality is a bit more complicated and complex than men's. An author on WebMD writes, *"Unlike men's main sexual complaint, erectile dysfunction, women's biggest sexual problem is caused by a combination of both mental and physical factors, which aren't likely to be cured by merely popping a pill."*

Women between the age 18 and 59, from reaching puberty to menopause, can start experiencing low sex drive. WebMD's article on the matter includes this really neat quote, "One of first things I do in speaking to women who come in with sexual concerns is let them know that there is no normal frequency or set of behaviors and things change with time," says Jan Shifren, MD, an assistant professor at Harvard Medical School. "If it's working for them and/or their partner, there is no problem."

See, this is part of the problem. We do not know how to quantify "high" and "low" sex drives. Every person has their own "norms" and "standards." Every couple will have their own system, their own norm. "But when a woman experiences a significant decrease in interest in sex that is having an effect on her life and is causing distress, then it's considered a problem of low sexual desire or HSDD."

Right? When it becomes problematic and starts causing you issues in the relationship, then it is time to start considering it a problem. "Kingsberg says that sexual desire is more than just an issue of low libido or sex drive. She says sexual drive is the biological component of desire, which is reflected as spontaneous sexual interest including sexual thoughts, erotic fantasies, and daydreams."

Kingsberg also raises an important point: sex drive decreases by age for a lot of people. "That sexual drive declines naturally with age based on physiological factors. But sexual desire also encompasses interpersonal and psychological factors that create a willingness to be sexual."

Then the article includes several reasons that women start to have low sex drive, "Interpersonal relationship issues. Partner performance problems, lack of emotional satisfaction with the relationship, the birth of a child, and becoming a caregiver for a loved one can decrease sexual desire. Sociocultural influences. Job stress, peer pressure, and media images of sexuality can negatively influence sexual desire.

Low testosterone: Testosterone affects sexual drive in both men and women. Testosterone levels peak in women's mid-20s and then steadily decline until menopause, when they drop dramatically.

Medical problems: Mental illnesses such as depression, or medical conditions, such as endometriosis, fibroids, and thyroid disorders, impact a woman's sexual drive both mentally and physically.

Medications: Certain antidepressants (including the new generation of SSRIs), blood pressure lowering drugs, and oral contraceptives can lower sexual drive in many ways, such as decreasing available testosterone levels or affecting blood flow.

Age: Blood levels of androgens fall continuously in women as they age."

Birth Control and Your Libido

It really depends on the medication you take. Some birth control pills lower sex drive, and others do not. It is all about side effects and individual bodies. Your body reacts to different chemicals in unique ways.

But, it seems like it is more likely that the birth control pill can cause lowering of your sex drive.

Lisa*, a 33-year-old Web designer from New York City, blames oral contraceptives for a year long libido malfunction she experienced after moving in with her now-husband. "When I realized I had no drive at all, I talked to my doctor, who said it was possible that it was the pill" causing the problem. "So I stopped taking it and used a barrier method, and things got really good again."'

Rodewald does not focus on Lisa alone, she writes about this issue being a common one, "Thirty percent of American women suffer from a diminished sex drive, and some experts (as well as non-experts) will tell you that the pill is often to blame. Studies have linked oral contraceptive use to decreased levels of androgens -- the class of hormones, including testosterone, thought to drive both male and female sexuality. Birth control pills also alter a woman's natural estradiol fluctuations (the group of hormones that includes estrogen), which many ob-gyns consider the main source of female libido. When you're on the pill, your hormonal balance changes -- and consequently, your desire for sex might change, too."

But, hang on, remember that every person is different and so it is natural that studies are not agreeing 100% on this issue. Rodewald reflects, "But don't throw out your pills just yet. Many studies have examined the effect of hormonal birth control on sex drive, but few have been conclusive, says Anne R. Davis, MD, MPH, assistant clinical professor of obstetrics and gynecology at Columbia University Medical Center in New York, who published a review of 40 years' worth of literature on contraceptive-libido studies. "

At epigee.org, there is a guide for the birth control pill and its effects on sex drives. The author explains, "It appears that the birth control pill affects sex drive because it acts directly on a woman's sexual hormones. In particular, the birth control pill inhibits the production of androgens, including testosterone, in a woman's ovaries. Androgens have a direct effect on the pleasure that you experience during sexual intercourse.

Additionally, the birth control pill also appears to increase the amount of sex-hormone binding globulin (SHBG) in the body. SHBG is a protein that binds to testosterone, preventing a woman's body from using it effectively. High levels of SHBG have been directly linked to decreased libido and sexual desire."
Just because it affects the sexual hormones does not mean that there is a decrease in it. It just means that it could be increased, decreased, or stay the same.

So How can you Increase Your Libido?

According to an article in Huffingtonpost.com, Shelley Emling writes, "In general, some 43 percent of women and 31 percent of men in the United States report sexual dysfunction. The numbers are even higher for those over 50. Indeed one study of menopausal women found that nearly half reported a decrease in sexual desire after menopause. Lots of issues contribute to the problem, including stress, smoking and hormonal imbalance." There are some ways you can increase your sex drive, though.

Aside from relaxing, changing medication, there are more solid ways to increase your sex drive naturally. "A study by Helen Fisher, an anthropologist at Rutgers University, found that when people look at a photo of their loved one for 30 seconds or longer, their brain begins producing dopamine, a libido booster. Of course, I know a lot of women who'd say that gazing at a photo of Ryan Gosling might be helpful as well."

Not only do you want to look your best, then, but you also need to stay fit for your sex drive naturally. "This one's mostly for men: Not only will you simply feel better about yourself, but body fat also inhibits testosterone production. And, apparently, it's really important for men to watch their waist size as belly fat absorbs testosterone more efficiently than fat cells elsewhere in the body. Both men and women will benefit from exercise, though, as aerobic workouts increase blood flow to sex organs"

Let us go back to relaxing, though, because it is really important to unwind: "No, you shouldn't drink to excess. And don't give up champagne completely. But studies show that moderate drinkers of red wine actually have a greater sex drive than those who don't imbibe, or who drink white wine. Researchers attribute this to red wine's ability to increase blood flow as well as its color. Women apparently find men a whole lot sexier when they are wearing red. And -- no surprise here -- men also are attracted to ladies in red."

Speaking of relaxing, "Certain scents are known to put people in the mood immediately (stock up on cinnamon, vanilla and musk in particular). An interesting side note: A woman's sense of smell is actually stronger than a man's, especially when she's ovulating. When it comes to men, apparently they get turned on by the scent of pumpkin pie combined with lavender. Who knew?"

Of course, I am going to be boring and say that communicating is also a natural way of increasing sex drives naturally. The more you share with your significant other, the better your sex life will be. And have fun: "Recent research shows that partaking in new and challenging experiences with your partner can boost the brain chemical dopamine, which helps fuel sex drive. These don't even need to be in the bedroom. Enter a race together, on a tandem bike. Get a little lost on a wilderness hike—without a map. Host a game night with friends where each couple kicks in $30 and the winning pair takes all," Deborah Kotz writes.

Libido When You are A couple

Sex ties and binds a couple together. It keeps them
close. Michele Weiner-Davis writes, "You have to

stop thinking you can have a great relationship without satisfying sex unless your partner wholeheartedly agrees. Don't resign yourself to passionless lovemaking or a relationship void of true intimacy. Even elderly and chronically ill people can enjoy a robust sex life."

So, how do you deal with someone who has a lower sex drive? Well, first, rule out any medical issues. Weiner-Davis explains, "To eliminate physiological causes for your lack of desire, a trip to your family physician or gynecologist may be in order. Ask if hormone replacement therapy such as testosterone would be appropriate. Evaluate whether side effects from medications or medical conditions are a factor in your situation. Discuss whether herbal remedies or dietary changes may be helpful."

Next, you may want to talk to a therapist to help you figure out if there is emotionally going on. Weiner-Dennis writes, "If you are a man whose sexual desire has plummeted due to your having sexual problems such as impotence or performance anxiety, a certified sex therapist can teach you many different techniques to overcome these difficulties.
It has been proven that regular and good exercise can among other benefits increase bloodflow to the

penis tissues for men thereby leading to improved sexual performance

Another natural way to increase libido is to get more used to eating Bananas, plantains and the NUTs such as Dates, coconuts, peanuts, tiger nuts and also yogurts. All of these food mentioned food items has over the years been proven helpful in increasing Libido level in both Men and Women.

You might also consider taking a drug such as Viagra, which will help you have and maintain an erection. I know it is really difficult for a man to admit he is worried about low sexual desire and even more difficult to ask for help in this area. But I urge you to do precisely that. You need to put your pride aside and get your sex life/marriage back on track. Your wife may understand at the moment, but if you put things off much longer, she might not be around."

Weiner-Dennis advises you to flirt, "If you think back to earlier times in your relationship, I bet the two of you were more flirtatious. I bet there were pats on the butt, a wink of your eye, a kiss blown across a crowded room, lightly touching each other in passing, a suggestive smile, a well-timed compliment about your spouse's appearance, and so on.

Either of you can initiate a conversation and talk about how romantically hot your first seven sexual intercourse you had together, in bet it was hot, mind-blowing, adventurous pleasurable as my own experience still linger in my head even as I write this book. This kind of playfulness is an important part of keeping passion alive. Put more energy into letting your spouse know that s/he is attractive by flirting."

Okay, so we got flirting, seeking medical and professional help. What else can you do to increase your sex drive? Weiner-Dennis explains, "Dr. Pat Love, coauthor of Hot Monogamy, suggests that it is frequently the case that people with low sexual desire never experience earth-shattering sexual urges as do their more sexually-oriented partners. For them, it's more like barely noticeable, mild tremors. Rather than assume that the Tidal Wave will be the cue that it's "sex time," look for more subtle signs"

And finally, you have to move, run: "Joggers always say that the hardest part about running is putting on your running shoes; so too with sex. I wish I had a dollar for every time I've heard a person say, "I really wasn't in the mood at all at first, but once we got into it, I enjoyed myself." My wife can testify to this. When people nudge themselves, even halfheartedly, to "get their feet moving," their pleasurable physical sensations often override any reason to resist."

Being Thrown into Menopause with Surgery

If you have to have a hysterectomy due to female issues this can really throw your body for a loop, especially if it is a total hysterectomy where they take out both of your ovaries.

Now your body is fighting you for the hormones it has been use to all these years that have been stripped away leaving you with nothing and this entire nothing? That leads to a low or nonexistent libido which of course is going to play havoc in your relationship.

Your partner won't understand why a surgery has taken your from yahoo to ya what in 2.5 seconds. They won't understand why you are tired all the time, why you can't even think about sex; when there isn't that "urge" there you just don't even care.

Know that you are not alone! Millions of women walk into their doctors office every year with a variety of complaints from aches and pains to lack of a sex drive or fatigue and most doctors don't even think about hormones they go right to their typical standbys, anti-anxiety meds, anti-depressants or a variety of medications to treat the symptoms.

If you have had a hysterectomy, are in menopause even if it has been years tell your Dr. you want your hormone levels checked!! I know of a woman who was one of these women who were given anti-anxiety meds and was on them for about 4 years before she read up about hormone replacement and all of the things in your body that are affected by your hormones!

She was 34 when she had a total hysterectomy, threw her into menopause immediately, was on a hormone patch for a couple years but it didn't really work too well. Hormones for women are a mix of Testosterone, Estrogen and Progesterone and all of these need to be at the right levels in order for you to feel your best!

Most Doctors don't have the perfect combination to give you and it's trial and error but there are those out there that will get your current levels and give you what you need to get to where you need to be and it is something that is inserted so you are never without! Once they know what you need and how often that is how often you will go in and get the pellets inserted.

She was going every 8 weeks, but everyone is different, some can go for months! Do yourself and your partner a favor and if you don't have a partner do it for you!! she did! she has been married for over 25 years and the difference between having the hormone replacement and not having it is like night and day!

Sex is sweet and it plays a vital role in every marriage, you do not have to starve your partner of sex, keep your home stay sexy.

Peace peace peace

www.ingramcontent.com/pod-product-compliance
Lightning Source LLC
Chambersburg PA
CBHW071458150726
48000CB00006B/2607